KT-230-860

EAT SMART
GRAINS

Louise Spilsbury

Heinemann
LIBRARY

www.heinemann.co.uk/library
Visit our website to find out more information about Heinemann Library books.

To order:
 Phone 44 (0) 1865 888066
 Send a fax to 44 (0) 1865 314091
 Visit the Heinemann Bookshop at www.heinemann.co.uk/library to browse our catalogue and order online.

Heinemann Library is an imprint of Capstone Global Library Limited, a company incorporated in England and Wales having its registered office at 7 Pilgrim Street, London, EC4V 6LB – Registered company number: 6695582

"Heinemann" is a registered trademark of Pearson Education Limited, under licence to Capstone Global Library Limited

Text © Capstone Global Library Limited 2009
First published in hardback in 2009
The moral rights of the proprietor have been asserted.

Edited by Charlotte Guillain and Diyan Leake
Designed by Richard Parker and Manhattan Design
Illustrated by Richard Parker (p. 16)
Picture research by Hannah Taylor
Production by Alison Parsons
Originated by Dot Gradations Ltd
Printed and bound in China by CTPS

ISBN 978 0 431066 17 2 (hardback)
13 12 11 10 09
10 9 8 7 6 5 4 3 2 1

British Library Cataloguing in Publication Data
Spilsbury, Louise
   Grains. - (Eat smart)
   641.3'31

A full catalogue record for this book is available from the British Library.

Acknowledgements
We would like to thank the following for permission to reproduce photographs: © Alamy pp. **13** (Rubberball), **20** (Dennis MacDonald); © Getty Images pp. **7** (The Image Bank/Karen Huntt), **8** (Stone/Gary Holscher), **9** (The Image Bank/Anthony Boccaccio), **12** (Photodisc), **15** (Riser/Sean Justice); © iStockphoto pp. **1–32** background images; © Pearson Education Ltd/MM Studios pp. **4**, **6**, **17**, **18**, **19**, **21**, **24**, **25** top, **25** bottom, **26**, **27** top, **27** bottom, **28**, **29** top, **29** bottom; © Photolibrary pp. **5** (Photononstop), **11** (imagebroker. net), **14** (Bob Winsett); © StockFood UK p. **10** (V. Muthuramann).

Cover photograph reproduced with permission of © Photolibrary (FoodCollection).

Every effort has been made to contact copyright holders of material reproduced in this book. Any omissions will be rectified in subsequent printings if notice is given to the publishers.

CONTENTS

Some words are shown in bold, **like this**. You can find out what they mean by looking in the glossary.

WHAT ARE GRAINS?

Grains are the **seeds** of cereal plants such as wheat, rice, maize (corn), and oats. Cereal plants belong to the grass family of plants. Like most other grasses, cereal plants usually have tall, flexible stems and long, thin leaves. The grains, or seeds, grow inside flowers at the top of a stem on a cereal plant.

Have people always eaten grains?

Thousands of years ago, people ate grains from wild plants. Then, between 11,000 and 15,000 years ago, people began to farm grain plants. The first grain crops were early forms of rice, wheat, rye, and barley. People first grew rice in East and South Asia, corn in Mexico, and oats in Germany. Gradually, as people explored and travelled, the different grains spread across the world.

 Today there are many different kinds of rice available, including white and wild rice, and also brown and even red rice.

Cereal plants, like these wheat plants, are members of the grass family. Like other kinds of grass, they have long, thin leaves.

Why is it smart to eat grains?

It is smart to eat grains because they are rich in **nutrients** that give the body **energy**. While cars run on petrol and computers are powered by electricity, people get energy from food. We use energy from grain foods to grow, stay healthy, and be active. You use more energy when you cycle or swim than you do when you sleep or watch TV, but even when you are not moving, your body still needs energy. It takes energy to keep your heart beating and your hair growing, for example.

A gift from the gods?

Early civilizations believed that each type of grain was a gift from the gods. In fact, the word "cereal" comes from Ceres, the name of the Roman goddess of grain. According to Ancient Egyptian legend, the goddess Isis brought the Egyptian people grains of barley and showed them how to grow it.

What kind of grains do people eat?

Some grains are sold and eaten whole. For example, people eat rice with main meals and add barley grains to stews and soups. Many grains are **processed** before you use them. Cracked grains, such as bulgur wheat, have been cut into smaller pieces so they cook more quickly. Grain flakes or rolled grains have been sliced and then flattened between rollers, as in rolled (porridge) oats and wheat or corn flakes.

This meal has been made with polenta. Polenta is yellow flour made by grinding up maize (corn) grains.

Bread and pasta

Wheat and other grains are often ground or crushed into the powder we call flour. Flour is used to make bread and pasta, so even though these foods look nothing like grains, they are grain foods. Pasta is made from flour and water and sometimes also eggs and oil. These are mixed into a paste and then dried and formed into pasta shapes, such as spaghetti and macaroni.

A staple food

A staple food is one that forms the main part of people's daily diet and supplies the bulk of their energy and nutrient needs. Grains are a staple food in many parts of the world. In South Asia rice is a staple food, and in some Asian countries people eat rice with every meal. In Central America maize, or corn, is a staple food. In central Asia and Mediterranean regions, wheat is the staple grain.

The big three

There are more than 50,000 **edible** plants in the world. Just three of these – rice, maize, and wheat – provide almost two-thirds of the energy people get from their food. These three grains are the staple foods for the majority of the world's population.

▲ The first breads people ever made, around 12,000 years ago, would have been flat breads rather like these tortillas.

WHERE DO GRAINS COME FROM?

Varieties of cereal plants grow in almost every part of the world. Different kinds of cereals grow best in different **climates**. Wheat and maize usually grow in places with mild climates. Oats and barley grow in cooler, damper climates. Rice can only grow in waterlogged soils, and some cereals such as millet grow well in hot, dry places.

A single wheat grain from a head of wheat like this can be ground into about 20,000 tiny pieces of flour!

What are cereal plants like?

Cereal plants are annuals. This means that unlike grass plants on a lawn, they do not live on year after year. To grow new cereal plants, farmers have to plant new **seeds** every year. After the seeds sprout, the plants grow and then make flowers. Cereal plant flowers are small, dull-coloured, and unscented feathery spikes. They do not have petals like most flowers in a garden. After the flowers have produced seeds, a cereal plant dies.

How does wheat grow?

To grow wheat, farmers in **temperate** climates plant seeds in late autumn. The plants start to develop in spring, when the temperature warms up and there is lots of rain. At this time, farmers may spray the plants with **fertilizers**, which help the plants grow and produce many seeds. By summer, wheat plants produce about 40 grains in every flower. The grain is harvested from July to September and then the cycle begins again.

Giant fields

Some of the biggest wheat fields in the world, such as those farmed in Canada or America, cover over 10,360 hectares (25,000 acres or 40 square miles).

Combine harvester machines like this cut off stalks of wheat and then separate off the grains. The leftover stalks of wheat – called straw – are also useful because they can be made into bales and used for animal feed or bedding.

How does rice grow?

In Asia, farmers plant rice seeds in soil beds. After one to two months, they transplant the young rice plants to rice or paddy-fields. These are fields that have been flooded by **monsoon** rains or filled with river water that has been channelled to the fields. When the rice grains are ready, farmers drain the water from the fields and harvest the crop by hand.

In some places, such as the United States, farmers may spray seeds onto waterlogged fields by aeroplane and monitor growth using computers. Machines keep fields wet by pumping a constant supply of water from wells or other water sources.

⬆ The hollow stalk of the rice plant soaks up water from the roots, which are planted in fields full of water.

From field to store

Rice grains are threshed, or cut from the rest of the plant, at harvest time. Any stones, dust particles, or bits of stalk are removed from the grains.

Then the grains are slowly dried by warm air. This reduces any moisture inside them, which would make them rot. Then the grains are **hulled** – this is when their tough outer skin, or **husk**, is removed.

Brown rice is **wholegrain** rice with only the husk removed. Some grains are further milled and polished to make white flour, or **processed** in some way – for example, ground up to make rice flour.

In many parts of the world, much of the work harvesting and threshing rice is done by hand or using small machines.

The amazing grain

There are about 140,000 different varieties of rice in the world and rice grows on every continent except Antarctica. About 90 percent of the world's rice is grown in Asia, where many people eat an average of half a kilogram (1 pound) of rice every day. Rice is used not only as food, but also for making rope, paper, cosmetics, packing material, and even toothpaste.

WHY ARE GRAINS GOOD FOR YOU?

Young plants use **nutrients** stored inside the **seed** to get the energy they need to grow. These energy-giving nutrients are **carbohydrates**. The grains that we eat are our main source of carbohydrates. Therefore they are our main source of energy.

How do carbohydrates work?

When you eat carbohydrates, your stomach and other parts of the **digestive system** break them down into **glucose**. Glucose is a kind of sugar. It moves into the bloodstream and the blood carries it to all parts of the body. Glucose from the blood passes into the body's **cells**. The body contains millions of cells and they are the body's basic building blocks. Inside each cell, glucose is mixed with **oxygen**. When glucose and oxygen react together, they release energy.

Carbohydrates provide you with the energy you need to be physically active. It also helps different parts of the body, such as the brain and heart, to work properly.

Digestive power

Did you know that your body starts digesting grains when you take your first bite? When you smell fresh-baked bread or see a plate of pasta, your mouth begins to produce saliva (spit). Saliva contains a substance called amylase, which starts to break down the carbohydrates in grains into glucose while you are chewing.

Having a reserve store of glucose in the form of glycogen means that the body has enough energy to keep going for long periods of time.

Energy stores

The body uses some of the glucose from carbohydrates to release energy right away. It also converts some of the glucose into **glycogen**, which can be stored in the **liver** or muscles. Any remaining glucose is stored in the fat cells as body fat. Later on, when your body needs more energy, it can change the glycogen or the body fat back into glucose. The glucose then goes back into your bloodstream and into the cells to give you an energy boost.

What are complex carbohydrates?

Complex carbohydrates are also known as **starchy** carbohydrates. Starchy carbohydrates include grains, foods made from grains such as bread and pasta, and potatoes. Foods with complex carbohydrates provide a slow and extended release of energy. They give you energy over a longer period of time and leave you feeling full for longer. This is why complex carbohydrates are the best source of energy.

 Carbohydrates provide you with the energy you need to be physically active. The body also uses this energy to make the brain and heart work properly.

What are simple carbohydrates?

Simple carbohydrates are sugars. Natural sugars are found in fruits, vegetables, and milk and dairy foods. The sugars used in fizzy drinks, sweets, and many prepared foods are **refined** sugars. Foods high in refined sugar release energy quickly, leaving you feeling hungry and tired soon after eating them. These foods also lack the nutrients found in complex carbohydrates.

Try to start
the day with
a breakfast
that includes
carbohydrate-
rich grains.

Do grains give other nutrients?

Grains contain B **vitamins** that help the body release energy from food and maintain a healthy **nervous system**. Folic acid, another B vitamin found in grains, helps the body form red blood cells. Grains also contain the **minerals** magnesium and selenium. Magnesium helps to build bones and make muscles work. Selenium helps protect cells and is important for a healthy **immune system**. Iron is used to carry oxygen in the blood.

Added goodness

Some foods made from grains have extra nutrients added to them. For example, some breads and breakfast cereals are enriched with other vitamins, such as vitamin D. Vitamin D helps maintain the body's level of calcium, a mineral used by the body to help maintain bones and teeth.

15

What are wholegrain foods?

A **wholegrain** food consists of the entire grain seed of a plant. A grain seed is made up of three key parts: the bran, the germ, and the endosperm (see picture below). A wholegrain can be a complete food, such as oatmeal, brown rice, and barley, or used as an ingredient in food, such as wholewheat or wholemeal flour in bread, pasta, crackers, and cereals.

What are refined grains?

Many grain foods are refined. This means they have been **processed** in factories that remove the bran and the germ. This makes them less chewy and quicker to cook than wholegrains. However, the bran and germ parts of a grain contain **fibre** and other nutrients such as vitamins. So, refined grain products, such as white rice, white bread, pasta, and many cereals, contain fewer nutrients and have less fibre than wholegrain foods.

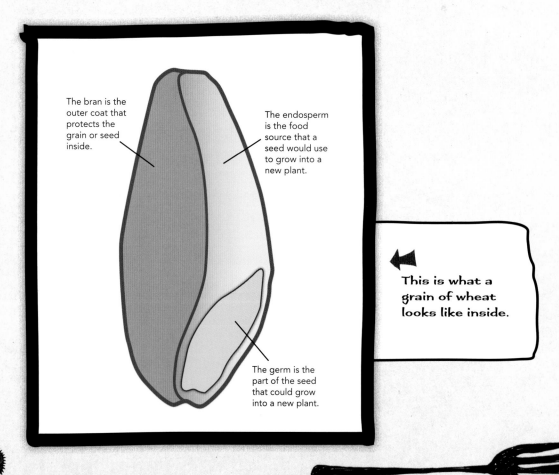

The bran is the outer coat that protects the grain or seed inside.

The endosperm is the food source that a seed would use to grow into a new plant.

The germ is the part of the seed that could grow into a new plant.

This is what a grain of wheat looks like inside.

◀ Choose wholegrains or foods that clearly state they contain whole oats, whole wheat, or whole rye on the label, to be sure you get the maximum fibre and nutrients in your daily diet.

Why do you need fibre?

Fibre is a part of food that passes through your digestive system relatively unchanged. However, it helps your body in other ways. Fibre-rich foods make you feel full, so you don't eat snacks and other foods that might make you overweight. Fibre also helps the **bowels** work properly. This prevents **constipation** and ensures waste does not linger in your body too long, which is unhealthy. Eating fibre-rich wholegrain foods also reduces the risk of heart disease.

Brown or wholegrain?

Some bread is made to look brown by adding substances such as molasses, but bread only contains all the nutrients of the wholegrain if it has wholewheat flour as the main ingredient. Look for the words "100 percent wholegrain bread" on the label.

WHAT IS THE BEST WAY TO EAT GRAINS?

 You can cook some grains, like this couscous, by combining them with boiling water. Couscous is made from ground wheat and is often used in salads or as a substitute for rice or pasta.

You can eat grains in a variety of ways. You can eat them for breakfast, add them to stews and soups, or use them in salads or side dishes. The most important thing is to eat a variety of grains, because each has different **nutrients**.

Cooking, keeping, and reheating

The fact that grains are dried means they keep for a long time before they are cooked. Different grains need to be cooked in different ways and for different lengths of time, so you need to read the packet instructions or a recipe. It is best to serve most grains just after they have been cooked.

After cooking, let leftover grains cool down before storing them in a sealed container in the fridge. Never leave cooked grains at room temperature for more than four hours. You can keep cooked grains for up to five days but do not reheat them more than once.

Store grain foods such as flours, millet, and rice in clean, dry, glass or ceramic containers with tight-fitting lids and put them in a cool, dark, dry place such as a cupboard. This keeps them fresh and safe to eat.

Ancient grains

Some nutritious grains that people ate long ago are coming back into fashion! Amaranth and quinoa were staple foods of the Incas of Peru and the Aztecs of Mexico. Amaranth is a tiny beige-coloured grain that can be used in baked foods such as bread and as a cereal. Quinoa (pronounced "keen-wa") is a small, round, brown grain you can cook as a substitute for rice. Use it as an ingredient in main meals and in place of oats to make a hot cereal.

Eating different grains

Try different grains prepared in different ways to find your favourites. The table below gives you some ideas.

Type of grain	Some ways to cook it
Brown rice	Try cooked cold rice in salads, hot cooked rice with stir fries, or baked rice in a sweet pudding.
Wheat	Cook wholewheat grains in casseroles. Add wheat germ and wheat bran to cakes or sprinkle it in baked dishes for extra nutrients.
Barley	Try using barley in place of rice – for example, in a risotto.
Millet	This grain is especially high in nutrients. Try mixing cooked millet with flavourings and mould into burgers.

 Corn grains can be eaten whole from a cooked cob like this, or you can use ground cornmeal flour to make breads or tortillas.

Ways to eat more wholegrains

There are many ways to eat more **wholegrains**. Replace a refined grain food you regularly eat with a wholegrain product – such as replacing white bread with wholewheat bread, or eating brown rice instead of white rice. For snacks, choose wholegrain cereal bars or wholegrain crisps such as baked tortilla chips. Popcorn is a healthy wholegrain snack if eaten with no added sugar, salt, or butter. Some wholewheat foods, such as wholewheat pasta, take longer to cook but they have a rich flavour.

Gladiators and grains

Gladiators of the Roman Empire were called "hordearii", meaning "barley men", because they ate so much barley. Gladiators ate barley to give them the strength, energy, and stamina they needed to fight each other in Roman amphitheatres for the amusement of the emperor.

Use wholegrains such as barley in a soup or stew.

A low-fat food

Grains are a naturally low-fat food. You need some fat to be healthy, but too much fat can make you overweight and put you at risk of health problems such as heart disease. Grain foods become unhealthy if served with too many sweet or fatty foods. Try putting less sauce on your rice or pasta, spread jam more thinly, and choose only one spread on your bread. Read the labels on prepared foods and choose those with few or no added sugars, fats, or oils.

HOW MUCH GRAIN SHOULD YOU EAT?

Grains are a vital part of a healthy diet. Different grains contain different amounts and kinds of **nutrients**, so to ensure you get the full range of nutrients that grains can offer, aim to eat a variety of different grains throughout the week.

Grain amounts

A healthy diet would include three to five servings of **carbohydrate** a day. One portion of carbohydrate is equivalent to:

- one slice of bread, one bread roll, or half a pitta bread
- six tablespoons of breakfast cereal or porridge
- four wholewheat crisp breads
- six tablespoons of pasta, rice, millet, or couscous.

Most of your grain foods should be **complex carbohydrates**. To ensure you get a balanced amount of carbohydrates, base each of your three main meals – breakfast, lunch, and dinner – on a complex carbohydrate such as brown rice, wholemeal pasta, or bread.

Top tip

Try to make at least half of all the grains you eat **wholegrains**, such as 100 percent wholewheat bread, brown rice, and oatmeal. You could try porridge oats for breakfast, a sandwich made with wholemeal bread for lunch, or a meal served with brown rice for dinner.

A balanced diet

Grains are good for us, but no single food contains all the essential **vitamins**, **minerals**, and nutrients we need to be healthy. A balanced diet is one that consists of a variety of foods from different food groups that together provide all the nutrients people need. The food plate diagram below shows the types and proportions of foods needed for a well-balanced diet. It shows how people should eat lots of fruit and vegetables, plenty of grains and other **starchy** carbohydrate foods such as bread, rice, pasta, and potatoes, some milk and dairy foods, some **proteins** such as meat, fish, eggs, and beans, and just a small amount of foods and drinks that are high in fat or sugar.

↑ If you want to eat smart and be healthy, try to think about the proportions of the different foods you eat in a day. See if you can match the proportions on this healthy food plate.

Grain recipes

Millet risotto

Risotto is usually made with rice. This millet version makes a nutritious lunch or dinner for two people.

Ingredients

- 300 g (10 oz) millet
- 2 red peppers
- 2 courgettes
- 1 onion
- 2 cloves of garlic
- 3 tomatoes
- 2 tablespoons grated cheese
- 2 tablespoons olive oil
- 1 tablespoon parsley
- Salt
- Nutmeg
- Pepper

Equipment

- Saucepan
- Large frying pan
- Measuring jug

WHAT YOU DO

1 Boil ½ litre (1 pint) of water and sprinkle in a teaspoon of salt. Put the millet in the boiling water, turn the heat down, and leave until cooked (about 20 minutes).

2 While the millet is cooking, prepare the vegetables. Peel and cut the onions and garlic into small pieces. Cut the red peppers and courgettes into small dice.

Always ask an adult to help you in the kitchen.

3 Heat the olive oil in a large frying pan over a medium to low heat. Add the onion and cook for a few minutes. Then add the chopped peppers, tomatoes, and courgettes.

4 After 10 minutes, add the cooked millet to the pan and stir.

5 Grate the cheese and chop the parsley finely. Add these to the pan and stir to mix.

6 Add salt, nutmeg, and pepper to taste. Serve while warm.

Tabouleh

This is a traditional salad from the Middle East. It combines bulgur wheat with salad vegetables and a dressing.

Ingredients

- 225 g (8 oz) bulgur wheat
- 450 ml (¾ pint) boiling water
- Half a cucumber
- 450 g (1 lb) tomatoes
- 6 spring onions
- 1 small bunch of flat leaf parsley
- 1 small bunch of mint
- 1 garlic clove
- 4 tablespoons olive oil
- 4 tablespoons lemon juice
- Salt and pepper

Equipment

- Large bowl
- Knife
- Chopping board
- Garlic crusher (optional)
- Clean jar with screw-top lid

WHAT YOU DO

1 In a large bowl, mix the bulgur wheat and 1 teaspoon salt together. Pour in the boiling water and leave for at least 15 minutes, until all the water has been absorbed.

2 Wash and chop the tomatoes and cucumber into small cubes. Cut off the roots and shoots from the spring onions. Chop the spring onions into small pieces. Finely chop the parsley and mint.

Always ask an adult to help when using tools such as sharp knives and blenders in a kitchen.

3 Add all the vegetables and herbs to the bulgur wheat and mix well.

4 Peel and chop (or crush) the garlic and put this into the jar together with the olive oil, lemon juice, and a small amount of salt and pepper. Screw the lid on tightly and shake the jar to mix the dressing. Pour the dressing over the salad and mix thoroughly.

5 You can serve the salad straight away or cover it and put it in the fridge for up to one day before serving.

Bread rolls

Making bread is not difficult and it is really satisfying to bake your own.

Ingredients

- 200 g (7 oz) plain flour
- 1 teaspoon salt
- 10 g (½ oz) powdered, easy-blend yeast
- 1 teaspoon sugar
- 150 ml (5 fl oz) warm water
- Butter, margarine, or oil to grease the tin

Equipment

- Loaf tin
- Sieve
- Mixing bowl
- Weighing scales
- Measuring jug
- Baking tray
- Oven gloves
- Cooling rack

WHAT YOU DO

1 Preheat the oven to 220 °C/ 425 °F/gas mark 7. Grease a loaf tin.

2 Sieve together the flour and salt into a mixing bowl.

3 Stir in the yeast and sugar.

4 Add the warm water and mix the ingredients. This is your dough.

5 Dust a little flour from the bag or jar onto the work surface and on your hands. This stops the dough sticking to your fingers too much. Then **knead** the dough for 10 minutes. To knead, make a ball out of the dough and press down on it with the heels of your hands (near your wrists). Stretch it out, fold it over, and press with your hands again. Repeat this over and over again. (Add more flour if needed, while you work.)

6 Divide the dough into four even pieces and shape the pieces into rolls.

7 Place the rolls on the greased baking tray.

8 Cover the dough and leave for 30 minutes in a warm place until it doubles in size.

9 Bake the rolls in the oven for 10–15 minutes until they are golden brown. Place on a rack to cool.

GLOSSARY

bowels part of the digestive system that prepares food for elimination from the body

calorie unit of energy contained in food and drink. Calories that are not used to produce energy are stored as fat.

carbohydrate type of nutrient found in food. The body breaks carbohydrates down into sugars that it uses for energy.

cell all living things are made up of millions of microscopic parts called cells. Different parts of the body are made up of different types of cells.

climate normal weather patterns of a region that occur year after year

complex carbohydrate nutrient that gives a slow release of energy to the body

constipation condition in which the movement of food through the digestive system is slower than normal, resulting in hard, dry stools that are uncomfortable to pass

digestive system stomach, intestine, and other body parts that work together to break down food into pieces so small they dissolve in liquid and pass into the blood

edible safe to eat

energy people require energy to be active and to carry out all body processes, including breathing

fertilizer substance that provides plants with nutrients that help them grow

fibre part of food which cannot be digested but helps to keep the bowels working regularly

glucose sugar that is the body's main source of energy

glycogen form in which glucose is stored in the body, mainly in the muscles and the liver

hulled has the outer covering of a fruit or seed removed

husk outer covering of some fruits and seeds

immune system the human body's system of defences against disease. The immune system includes white blood cells and antibodies that react against bacteria and other harmful material.

knead work dough by pressing and folding it with the hands

liver body part located inside the body, below the chest. The liver cleans the blood and produces bile, a substance that helps break down food in the digestive system.

mineral substance that comes from non-living sources, such as rocks that break down and become part of the soil. Some of the nutrients that plants take in through their roots are called minerals.

monsoon seasonal wind that brings heavy rainfall to places such as India and southern Asia

nervous system system of nerves that regulates and coordinates all the body's activities

nutrient substance found in food that is essential for life

oxygen a gas in the air

processed prepared or treated in a particular way, generally with the use of machinery

protein nutrient that provides the raw materials the body needs to grow and repair itself

refined grains that have been processed by machines that remove some of their natural substances, such as the bran and the germ

seed plant part that can grow into another plant. Most plants make flowers, which eventually turn into fruit. The seeds are inside the fruit. Seeds can be spread by wind, water, or animals.

simple carbohydrate nutrient that gives a quick, short-lived release of energy to the body

starchy something containing starch. Starch is a plant's store of excess glucose (food).

temperate climate that has warm summers and cold winters

vitamin nutrient people require to grow and stay healthy

wholegrain the entire grain seed of a plant. Wholegrains contain more nutrients and fibre than refined grains, which have some of the grain seed removed.

FIND OUT MORE

At **www.eatwell.gov.uk** there is a wide range of information, including tips on eating healthy foods and keeping food safe.

The BBC website **www.bbc.co.uk/health/healthy_living/nutrition** covers many aspects of healthy eating.

At **kidshealth.org/kid** there is a large section on staying healthy and some recipes to try.

Click on the 'Healthy eating' link at **www.nutrition.org.uk** for ideas for healthier lunches, a closer look at the Eatwell plate, and more.

INDEX